THE EVOLUTION OF Insects

by Christine Evans

Content Consultant

Heath Blackmon
Assistant Professor
Department of Biology
Texas A&M University

Essential Library

An Imprint of Abdo Publishing | abdobooks.com

ANIMAL EVOLUTION

abdobooks.com

Published by Abdo Publishing, a division of ABDO, PO Box 398166, Minneapolis, Minnesota 55439.

Printed in the United States of America, North Mankato, Minnesota.
092018
012019

Cover Photo: Klaus Mohr/Shutterstock Images
Interior Photos: iStockphoto, 4–5, 9 (bee), 18–19, 22, 31, 37, 42, 51, 62–63, 65, 70–71, 73, 81, 82, 89, 97; Guillermo Guerao Serra/Shutterstock Images, 6; Shutterstock Images, 9 (chart), 13, 45, 56–57; Ian Redding/iStockphoto, 10, 77; Cathy Kiefer/iStockphoto, 11; Igor Zarembo/Sputnik/AP Images, 16; Malcolm Schuyl/FLPA/Science Source, 20; The Natural History Museum, London/Science Source, 23, 40; N. Nehring/iStockphoto, 27; Barnaby Chambers/iStockphoto, 28–29; Andrew Paul Deer/Shutterstock Images, 33; Dr. Morley Read/Shutterstock Images, 35; Mark Brandon/Shutterstock Images, 38, 46; Danté Fenolio/Science Source, 47; OG Photo/iStockphoto, 52–53; Sandra Standbridge/Shutterstock Images, 55; Irakli Shavgulidze/Shutterstock Images, 60; Innovus Photography/Shutterstock Images, 61; ER Degginger/Science Source, 64; Banks Photos/iStockphoto, 67; Kanchana Tuihun/Shutterstock Images, 69; Selma Caparroz Barros/Shutterstock Images, 74; Christian Ziegler/Minden Pictures/Newscom, 76; R. T. Bilder/Shutterstock Images, 78; Mark Harmel/Science Source, 85; Eileen Kumpf/iStockphoto, 86; Dr. Paul A. Zahl/Science Source, 90–91; Pascal Goetgheluck/Science Source, 93, 99

Editor: Marie Pearson
Series Designer: Becky Daum

Library of Congress Control Number: 2018947968

Publisher's Cataloging-in-Publication Data

Names: Evans, Christine, author.
Title: The evolution of insects / by Christine Evans.
Description: Minneapolis, Minnesota : Abdo Publishing, 2019 | Series: Animal evolution | Includes online resources and index.
Identifiers: ISBN 9781532116650 (lib. bdg.) | ISBN 9781532159497 (ebook)
Subjects: LCSH: Insects--Evolution--Juvenile literature. | Animal evolution--Juvenile literature. | Biological evolution--Juvenile literature. | Insects--Juvenile literature.
Classification: DDC 574.30--dc23

CONTENTS

Bumblebees spread pollen from flower to flower, enabling plants to reproduce.

CHAPTER ONE

Incredible Insects

Insects are the most varied of all invertebrates—animals without backbones—and are essential to life on Earth. They pollinate fruit trees and break down dead plants and animals to make soil. Other animals eat insects as a vital part of their diets. There are more than one million known insect species crawling, swimming, and flying in environments from tropical rain forests and deserts to rivers and swamps as well as in backyards and bedrooms all over the planet.[1] But there could be at least two million insect species still unidentified.[2] Insects range from beautiful dragonflies and butterflies to scavenging ants and fruit flies, but they all share the same characteristics. They have an external skeleton, or exoskeleton;

Scientists have found many trilobite fossils.

three pairs of legs; a segmented body including a head, thorax, and abdomen; and one pair of antennae. Most adult insects also have wings.

BEFORE BUGS

Half a billion years ago there were no insects. Planet Earth looked very different. On land, there were no animals. Nothing flew in the sky. No trees, flowers, or grass grew. But in the ocean, life was abundant. Algae floated on the ocean surface, providing food for the marine life below. Strange creatures called trilobites looked like giant pill bugs. They lurked on the muddy seafloor in the shallow water alongside sea snails, starfish, and sea urchins. Massive eurypterids, or sea scorpions, grew up to six feet (2 m) long and terrorized the sea.[3] Eurypterids hunted for prey by grabbing it with their powerful claws. They were the top of the food chain in a world where there were no vertebrates—animals with backbones—to compete with. The period of life on Earth when these animals evolved, beginning approximately 541 million years ago (MYA), is called the Cambrian explosion. Prior to the explosion, there were no animals with legs or eyes. There were no predators. Primitive multicelled organisms floated through the water, passively absorbing nutrients. Scientists studying oxygen levels in prehistoric rocks believe there may have been a small increase

CAMBRIAN EXPLOSION

Life on Earth began 3.8 billion years ago when the first molecules capable of replication developed. But it wasn't until the Cambrian explosion 541 MYA that life took off. It's described as an explosion because many new species of animals evolved in a relatively short period of time. But despite its name, this evolution didn't happen in a flash. The Cambrian explosion lasted ten million years.

Because many fossils have been discovered from this period of time, scientists believe there was an evolutionary explosion. Before this period, the fossil record was sparse. Fossils found in the Burgess Shale—a fossil deposit in what is now British Columbia, Canada—from 505 MYA show creatures recognizable as arthropods and worms. So a rapid period of evolution must have occurred by then. The Burgess Shale used to be 670 feet (200 m) underwater.[4] The deposit formed 515 MYA when underwater mudslides swept creatures over a cliff and instantly buried them, creating fossils. As well as preserving hard-shelled arthropods, the rapid burial preserved soft-bodied creatures that usually decomposed.

in available oxygen. This caused more predators to evolve, so their prey also had to evolve quickly to adapt and survive in a world where they could be hunted and eaten. Scientists believe most of the animals alive on Earth today descend from the creatures that evolved during the Cambrian explosion.

ARTHROPODS MOVE TO LAND

Trilobites and sea scorpions are classified as part of a group of animals called arthropods. Scientists split up the known animal kingdom into groups called phyla. The animals in the Arthropoda phylum have segmented bodies, jointed legs, and hard exoskeletons that protect them like armor. The Arthropoda phylum is further split into several different groups called classes. Crustaceans such as crabs and lobsters make up one class. Spiders are in the Arachnida class. And insects make up the Insecta class. Within each class are different orders. For instance, the order Lepidoptera within the insect class contains all the butterflies and moths.

Approximately 500 MYA, the first plants made their way onto land. Algae started to grow on shores, taking root and becoming rigid enough to stand upright and collect more sunlight. Algae continued to develop into green mosses, ferns, and horsetails. These early plants provided homes and food for the first creatures that also moved from water to land. The early land

CLASSIFICATION

Honey Bee

Apis mellifera

DOMAIN	**Eukaryota**. This domain includes plants, animals, and fungi. These organisms are grouped together because their cells each have a nucleus, a cell structure that contains the DNA.
KINGDOM	**Animalia**. All animals, including mammals and insects, are in this group.
PHYLUM	**Arthropoda**. Organisms in this phylum have an exoskeleton and segmented bodies.
CLASS	**Insecta**. This class contains insects, whose bodies have three segments: the head, thorax, and abdomen. They also have three pairs of legs that they use for walking.
ORDER	**Hymenoptera**. This order contains insects including ants, bees, sawflies, and wasps.
FAMILY	**Apidae**. Bees make up this family.
GENUS	***Apis***. This family contains nine bee species that may all at times be called honey bees.
SPECIES	***mellifera***. Honey bees are the only domestic species of bee. They are the only species of the genus Apis that lives outside of Asia.

Taxonomic classification is the science of identifying living things, grouping them together, and naming them. When this is done, each organism is assigned a place in eight different categories ranging from domain, the most general category, to species, the most specific category. When the scientific name of an animal is given, it includes the genus, which is capitalized, and the species, which is not. Honey bees are *Apis mellifera*. Scientific names are often abbreviated after first use: *A. mellifera*.

SPRINGTAILS

Springtails may have been some of the earliest land dwellers. These small, wingless arthropods may have originally crawled out of the water to reproduce away from predators and to seek a hiding place in the algae. Springtails got their name because of the taillike appendage they use for leaping. They're so similar to insects that scientists used to believe they were closely related, but recent DNA studies put them in their own order. They probably made the transition from ocean to land before insects.

explorers may also have been avoiding large predators, such as sea scorpions, that preferred to hang out in deeper water. Arthropods were well equipped for life on land in prehistoric times. Their exoskeletons helped protect them from the sun. Their jointed legs propelled them onto land.

The evolution of insects occurred in four episodes, or stages, that happened over millions or even tens of millions of years. The first episode of insect evolution was when the early insect ancestors, which resembled modern bristletails (from the order Archaeognatha), evolved. The second stage was when some insects evolved wings that can't fold, such as those on dragonflies. Later, other insects evolved wings that could fold, such as those

Butterflies develop through complete metamorphosis. Caterpillars undergo a drastic transformation into their adult forms.

on cockroaches. The fourth stage of evolution was the evolution of complete metamorphosis, the transformation of the animal as it develops to an adult form. One example of this is the transformation of caterpillars to butterflies. Finally, social groups developed. For example, ants or bees live and work together in groups to find food and rear their young.

Metamorphosis is a process that benefits insects by allowing them to have significantly different life stages to avoid competition for habitats and food sources within a species. Not all insects use metamorphosis in the growth and development process, and some only use incomplete metamorphosis. However, all animals with an exoskeleton must shed their skin to grow, which is why different insects have varying levels of metamorphosis. Insects from the fourth stage of evolution have complete metamorphosis, which includes three life stages: larva, pupa, and adult. The different life stages use energy efficiently for a specific goal. This allows the insects to transition rapidly through their life cycles. A larva, such as a caterpillar, may look completely different from the adult form. The larva spends most of its time eating and growing. During the pupal stage, the pupa is inactive. Its body, often encased in a protective covering, changes from the larval form to the adult form. Adults emerge from the pupal stage ready to find a mate and reproduce.

On the other hand, insects from the first stage of evolution do not participate in any metamorphosis. Often, the juvenile insects look very similar to the adults, and the main distinction is whether or not the sex organs are functional. Then, there are insects from the second and third stages of evolution. Some take part in incomplete metamorphosis, with pronymph, nymph, and adult stages. The pronymph stage may largely happen while in the egg. A pronymph is generally helpless and does not actively feed but lives off of the nutrients from its yolk. Nymphs typically look similar to their adult forms, but they cannot reproduce. They eat and change as they grow into adults. Sometimes the physical function between the nymph and adult stages of an insect are so different that the insect must develop a completely different

A dragonfly nymph bears some resemblance to its adult form.

form as it grows. Scientists believe the pronymph, nymph, and adult stages later evolved into the more efficient stages of larva, pupa, and adult in some groups.

Evolution is defined as genetic changes in organisms across generations. All organisms alive today, and those that are extinct, are connected. Genetic changes come about as mutations in the DNA. Genetic mutations—random changes in the animal's DNA—can occur throughout an organism's life. The mutations won't affect the future population unless they change the animal's chance of survival. Natural selection can then act on these mutations. For instance, if a mutation leads to a trait that increases reproduction or survival, animals will reproduce and pass on that trait to their offspring. Over time, the trait that allows animals to survive and reproduce will become more common.

HOW FOSSILS FORM

Fossils form when an animal is rapidly buried in sediment. All the soft parts of the animal rot away, leaving behind the hard material, such as the exoskeleton. Eventually, minerals permeate the remains and harden, turning into rock. There are two different types of fossils found in rock: body fossils and trace fossils. Body fossils preserve the body parts of an animal. Trace fossils record the marks that animals made, such as footprints.

Another form of fossilization happens when animals get trapped in amber. Amber forms when tree bark is punctured and the resin oozes out. Insects get stuck in the resin. If the droplets get buried in sediment, they eventually harden and form fossils. The soft tissue of ancient animals sometimes has been preserved in amber, and the resulting fossils give scientists a valuable window into life millions of years ago.

During the first stage of insect evolution, the earliest wingless insects appeared. An early insect that ate the new plants was the bristletail. Bristletails are considered the most ancient of living insects and still exist in diverse habitats all around the world today. In 1988, scientists in Canada discovered fossils that dated to more than 390 MYA. These fossils included bristletails. At the time, they were the oldest insect fossils ever discovered.

The age of fossils can be figured out by examining the layer of rock the fossils are found in. When rock forms, it builds up in horizontal layers called strata. The deeper the fossils are found, the older they are. Fossils from the same location can be compared in age based on how deep they lie. However, fossils from different locations can't be compared this way. So scientists use other techniques to figure out how old a fossil is. One technique is to compare fossils found in the same layer—if scientists know when the species went extinct, they can figure out the age of the other fossils around it. Radiometric dating—determining the age of rocks by measuring how radioactive materials in those rocks change over time—can also be used to determine the age of the rock layer.

Another early insect looked like modern silverfish (from the order Zygentoma). Silverfish are those silver, wiggling insects that invade kitchens today. Silverfish that live in human habitats eat tasty kitchen crumbs in addition to the lichens and algae they may have eaten when their ancestors first evolved.

RECENT FOSSIL EVIDENCE

Scientists examine fossils to figure out when certain animals first roamed the earth. The oldest insect fossil is thought to be 400 million years old. It is of an insect named *Rhyniognatha hirsti*. The fossil had lingered in a vault at London's Natural History Museum since the 1920s until two entomologists, Michael Engel and David Grimaldi, took a new look at it in 2004. They used a modern microscope to examine the specimen and were astonished by what they saw—they could see a type of mouthpart that usually only appears in flying insects. So they concluded that

Some insects were fossilized in amber, which forms from ancient tree resin.

insect flight had evolved at least 400 MYA. Before the discovery, scientists believed insects had started flying 320 MYA.

A prehistoric insect fossil discovered in 2012 is thought to be from around 360 MYA. This fossil was nearly complete—a first for this period in Earth's early history. The insect was recognized as a new species and named *Strudiella devonica*. However, a group of scientists disputed the claim that this fossil was an insect. It can be difficult interpreting fossils. This means scientists might not be able to accurately tell what type of animal a fossil is. There are also big gaps in fossil records because fossils only form under certain conditions. Additionally, just because one insect looks like another does not mean that they are closely related. Recent technological advances mean that scientists studying evolution can use DNA evidence instead of appearance to construct insect family trees.

DNA EVIDENCE

In 2014, a team of more than 100 scientists published a study revealing the origins of insects and how they are related to each other and the other classes in the phylum Arthropoda. The group studied 1,478 genes from insects and other arthropods to determine how insects evolved.[5] The study revealed that insects descended from crustaceans, another branch of the arthropods. Insects are related to crustaceans known as remipedes. Remipedes are blind, long-bodied cave dwellers that still exist today. Because of the close relationship, scientists believe the ancestor of all insects may have resembled ancient and modern remipedes.

Scientists know from fossil and DNA evidence that all the insects living today descended from the same group of animals. They have evolved to live all over the world. They have different characteristics, habitats, and predators. Eventually, an event helped propel insects to world domination today, when 80 percent of the world's species are insects.[6] This event was the second stage of insect evolution: the development of wings.

Damselflies are generally smaller than dragonflies. They can have stunning colors.

CHAPTER TWO

Dragonflies and Damselflies

If you watch a dragonfly hover like a helicopter by a river or lake, it's like looking more than 300 million years into the past. The dragonflies' form has hardly changed since these prehistoric fliers first evolved. Dragonflies fly and rest with their wings held out—they aren't able to fold them away as butterflies and beetles can. Dragonflies and damselflies live by fresh water, the perfect spot to catch mosquitoes or butterflies to eat. They can see almost 360 degrees to spot their prey before catching it mid-flight, mashing it with their strong jaws.[1]

Dragonflies might lay their eggs on partially submerged plants.

For most of their lives, dragonflies and damselflies live underwater. When a dragonfly or damselfly nymph—also called a larva—hatches from its underwater egg, it has no wings. But the nymph is a ferocious predator, gobbling up small fish, tadpoles, or even other nymphs with its powerful mouthparts. Nymphs have gills to take in oxygen underwater. They can stay in this stage for several years before emerging as adults. As the nymphs grow, they molt their hard exterior shells several times, growing a little more each time until they're ready for their final molt. When the time comes to fly, the nymph climbs out of the water and onto a reed.

The dragonfly then breaks free of its old skin and unfurls its new wings. It has two pairs, and liquid from its body pumps down veins in the wings to stretch them tight. The sun dries the wings until they're hard enough to fly. As adults, some dragonflies only live for a few weeks. At most, an adult dragonfly will live one year.

THE DEVELOPMENT OF WINGS

The first insects on the planet were wingless and walked on six legs along the ground. So where did wings come from? No one knows for sure, because the fossil record can be incomplete and hard to interpret. Since the 1800s, scientists have been discussing theories about how insects developed the ability to fly.

The gill theory says wings evolved from gills, like the gills that dragonfly nymphs have. But another theory is that the wings developed from lobes attached to the insect's thorax. One of the earliest fossils of a winged insect supports this second theory. The 325-million-year-old fossil is of an insect from a now-extinct order of insects called Palaeodictyoptera. The Palaeodictyoptera were among the first winged insects on the planet. These enormous insects had wings up to 22 inches (56 cm) wide.[2] They made up approximately 50 percent of the insects on Earth at the time.[3] The Palaeodictyoptera had unusual mouths for insects. They had beaks.

Nymphs shed their exoskeletons several times as they grow until they finally reach their adult size.

They used the beaks to pierce plants and suck up their contents. This order of giant insects vanished approximately 250 MYA during a major extinction event that killed 70 percent of life on land.[4]

Palaeodictyoptera weren't directly related to dragonflies, but their fossils may help explain the origins of flight. The prehistoric fossils show a pair of lobes as well as two pairs of wings. The theory is that the Palaeodictyoptera nymph had three pairs of veined lobes, enabling it to warm up and become active quickly. Extended lobes enabled the insect to glide so it could escape predators. The final step to complete the evolution of wings was for the insect to develop the necessary muscles so two pairs of wings could be flapped. Scientists once believed

FOSSILS OF EARLY WINGED INSECTS

It's rare to find a complete fossil of a winged insect (pictured). That's because the bodies of flying insects are soft and fragile, and predators often eat them. Paleontologists often find only the remains of wings, which are not digested easily. But in 2008, Richard Knecht, a scientist from Harvard University, found a complete mayfly fossil in a marsh behind a strip mall in Massachusetts. Mayflies have long, thin bodies with straight wings like those of dragonflies. The fossil was an impression of an ancient mayfly and was probably made when the mayfly rested in the mud and got stuck.

Palaeodictyoptera was the original winged insect that all other flying insects evolved from. More recent studies dispute this theory.

Another possible origin of wings is from insects' legs. The ancient ancestors of insects had multiple segments and many pairs of legs. The theory is that one of these pairs of legs evolved to become wings.

Modern scientists can use DNA and can even manipulate insects' genes in a laboratory to discover answers to some of evolution's puzzles. A 2018 study suggests the origin of wings was a combination of these ideas—the lobes on the insects' backs combined with the articulation of the legs created the wings seen today on dragonflies and other flying insects. Scientists reached this conclusion by genetically modifying beetle larvae so that they grew a third set of wings on their abdomens. They used a fluorescent green protein that they introduced to the beetles' genes to see where the new wing development originated from—green appeared both on the insects' backs and in the area where their legs originated. Yoshinori Tomoyasu, one of the scientists who studied the beetles, said, "We are very confident about our analyses, but it's a prediction. It would be very cool to actually see the shape of an ancestral insect."[5] Until fossils are found that show a certain origin of wings, scientists can only theorize about how insects began to fly.

FLIGHT AND THE EVOLUTION OF PLANTS

Flight was helpful for insects for many reasons. There were few predators in the skies, so if there was a threat, insects could take flight and seek out somewhere else to live. Insects could colonize new areas that hadn't yet been inhabited and where there was less competition for food. The evolution of wings allowed for new adaptations, including the ability to act as camouflage, to act as protection, to make sound, and to regulate body temperature. For example, a stick insect's wings look like leaves. A beetle's folded wings protect its abdomen. Male crickets use their wings to chirp and attract female crickets. And dragonflies use their wings to catch sun to warm them up and make them

THE GRIFFINFLY

A distant relative of dragonflies was the largest-known insect ever to take to the skies. Its name was *Meganeuropsis*, commonly called the griffinfly. Fossils of this insect were first described by Frank Carpenter in 1939. Carpenter estimated its wingspan measured a gigantic 30 inches (75 cm) across.[6] Scientists believe an increase in oxygen levels during the time the griffinfly was alive 300 MYA was responsible for the gigantic size of the predatory insects. Insects don't have lungs. They distribute oxygen around their bodies through a system of narrow tubes. This system, coupled with their hard exoskeletons, means modern insects can't grow very large. But the griffinflies didn't have that problem thanks to the increased oxygen. Oxygen levels in the atmosphere reached 30 percent. Today levels are at 21 percent.[7]

The griffinfly died out at the end of the Permian period (298.9–251.9 MYA) during the mass extinction. Oxygen levels later decreased, so no other insect has reached the griffinfly's size since. The rise of birds also influenced insects' small size. When birds evolved and took to the skies, they preyed on large insects. It became an advantage to be small and nimble to escape predatory birds.

THE GREAT PERMIAN-TRIASSIC EXTINCTION

Approximately 250 MYA, something killed approximately 96 percent of marine species and 70 percent of life on land.[8] Thirty percent of all insect species became extinct.[9] Every animal alive on Earth today is descended from the surviving species. There are many theories about what caused the extinction, including an asteroid impact, a release of the gas methane, a drop in oxygen levels, sea level fluctuations, or maybe a combination of events. There have been other mass extinctions during Earth's history, including the one that famously caused the demise of dinosaurs, but the great Permian-Triassic extinction was the only one that affected insects.

ready to fly. Dragonfly wings can also shield their bodies to help them cool down.

From 416 to 358 MYA, the number of plants on the planet started to increase. Plants release oxygen, so an increase in plants meant more oxygen available to the creatures inhabiting the planet. Scientists believe that this allowed for the evolution of more complex animals, such as winged insects. Plants were also growing taller. They developed into forests. Food sources that other animals couldn't reach were now available to the flying insects. Forests also provided safety from predators.

Dragonfly wings are an example of the second stage of wing evolution. They hold their wings straight out. But later, other insects developed the ability to fold their wings away.

Dragonflies use their wings to help regulate their body temperature.

Some cockroaches are attracted to human dwellings because of the crumbs of food that fall to the floor.

CHAPTER THREE

Cockroaches, Termites, and Mantises

Cockroaches, termites, and mantises make up the Dictyoptera order of insects. Cockroaches have a terrible reputation as kitchen invaders, but there are approximately 4,600 species living in forests, mountains, and swamps all over the world.[1] They have leathery front wings that they fold back to protect their back wings. Their strong jaws can munch through most foods, including grass, leaves, and dead wood.

AVOIDING TRAPS

Approximately 30 years ago, pest-control companies started mixing sugary food with insecticides—chemicals that kill cockroaches and other insects. However, by 1993, the poison seemed to stop working. The cockroaches had evolved to ignore the glucose—a form of sugar—in the bait. This response to glucose could have stemmed from two causes. After the use of poisons began, individual cockroaches may have had a mutation that led them to avoid glucose. Or this trait already existed in cockroaches. Either way, those that avoided glucose were more likely to survive and pass on the trait to their offspring. Scientist Coby Schal has a theory on how this trait may have evolved in cockroaches. He notes that certain plants make substances that are toxic and taste bittersweet. Even before people began putting out poison, cockroaches would have needed to avoid this flavor in order to survive. As people built homes, cockroaches moved in and may have developed an interest in sugar so they could feed on food crumbs that fell to the floor. Then, when people put out poison that had sugar, the trait that causes cockroaches to avoid sugar possibly came back.

Termites are famous for their giant homes, which can reach up to 30 feet (9 m) tall in South Africa.[2] But they live all over the world, including in North America, Europe, and tropical rain forests in South America and Asia. Termites are known for causing damage to houses by chomping through wood—an essential part of their diet.

Mantids, also known as praying mantises, are slow-moving insects named for their hunting stance with their front legs folded up in front of them. This stance makes them look like they are praying. Mantises eat live insects such as moths and crickets. They spot their prey by turning their heads 180 degrees to scan their surroundings while staying still and camouflaged in the undergrowth.[3] The females

People are most familiar with green mantises, but mantises come in other colors, too.

have another kind of meal—the male mantis, which they devour after mating. The females then lay hundreds of eggs. The young mantises hatch looking like tiny versions of their parents.

EVOLUTION OF COCKROACHES AND TERMITES

Ancient cockroaches roamed the planet when all the land on Earth was joined together in a supercontinent called Pangaea. The first fossils of these prehistoric cockroaches date from 318 to 315 MYA. Cockroaches are part of the third episode of insect evolution—the development of folding wings. The transition from insects such as dragonflies, which rest with their wings extended from the body, to insects such as cockroaches, which fold their wings flat against their bodies, required changes in the way the wings were hinged. The wings also evolved so that when they're folded away, they don't stick out and get damaged. Scientists studied the DNA of insects to discover how their wings changed. They believe that a gene called Ultrabithorax is responsible for the different wing sizes and shapes among insects.

Scientists were able to determine that termites evolved from cockroaches by several means. The two share several features, including specialized cases that enclose their eggs, similar-looking young, and the same perforations in the internal parts of their heads. But it wasn't until 2007, when scientists studied the DNA sequences of 107 different species of termites, cockroaches, and mantises from

GIANT HOMES

In the animal kingdom, termites build among the tallest non-human structures in proportion to their body size. Cathedral termites build huge mounds up to 26 feet (8 m) high in western Australia.[4] The ancestors of these termites used to build their nests in trees, but later they began building mounds on the ground and eating grass instead of wood. The scale of these structures in relation to the size of termites is enormous. If termites were human sized, their giant homes would be the same size as four Burj Khalifas (the tallest building in the world in 2018) stacked on top of each other. That's 10,866 feet (3,312 m) tall.[5]

Cathedral termites build very large mounds to live in.

across the globe, that they were able to confirm their idea.[6] In DNA sequencing, scientists can see where an animal's DNA is the same as another animal's and where it's different. The more the DNA matches, the closer the specimens are related. Termites and wood-eating cockroaches, *Cryptocercus punctulatus*, can trace their lineages back to a common ancestor 251 MYA. The wood-eating cockroach lives inside rotten logs. These cockroaches also live in groups, like termites. And fossil termite nests found in Arizona rocks from 220 MYA showed that termites were chewing wood and making nests at that time, just like the wood-eating cockroach does today. Scientists believe wood-eating cockroaches and termites evolved to eat wood by consuming microbes from the droppings of their relatives. These microbes help them break down wood. To ensure those microbes get passed on to future generations, the offspring need to stay close to their parents in the social group.

Ants and bees may be the first insects that come to mind when thinking of insects living in social groups, but termites did it first. In fact, scientists believe termites evolved 100 million years before any other social insect.

TERMITES TIPTOE TO AVOID ANTS

Ants often eat termites, but termites have evolved a way to avoid being detected by ants. Termites tiptoe. Ants hunting just millimeters away from their prey don't even notice their dinner foraging nearby. Termites are blind, but they have evolved super-sensitive hearing so that when they detect ants nearby, they start treading lighter and dodge out of the way. They're so good at it that scientists wonder if replicating the sound of ant footsteps could be a solution to chemical-free termite control. People could place devices that mimic the sound of ant footsteps around houses to deter these pests.

EVOLUTION OF SOCIAL GROUPS

In natural selection, small changes that lead to a greater chance of survival get passed on to subsequent generations. But in social species

Termites work together to build homes and care for young.

of animals such as termites, ants, and bees, most members of the colony cannot have offspring. Instead they act as workers hunting for food or soldiers defending the colony. Scientists asked what the advantage is of having a large number of offspring that never reproduce, find mates, or start their own colonies. Charles Darwin, who wrote *On the Origin of Species* in 1859 and first described evolution and natural selection, called the evolution of social groups, "the one special difficulty, which at first appeared to me insuperable and actually fatal to my whole theory."[7] Researcher and University of Maryland evolutionary biologist Barbara Thorne spent nearly 30 years pursuing the answer to this mystery. Her theory is that it was more advantageous for early termite offspring to stay home to help their parents rather than risk creating independent colonies. The young termites would then take over the colony when their parents died.

MANTISES

As with termites, the mantises also likely evolved from cockroaches—specifically a praying mantis–like cockroach called *Manipulator modificaputis* that caught and ate prey, unlike modern cockroaches. An example of this species of cockroach was found in a 100-million-year-old amber fossil in Burma. The insect had a long neck, which gave it the ability to rotate its head freely, and unusually long legs, which led researchers to conclude that it actively pursued prey. During the early Cretaceous period (145–66 MYA), several predatory cockroach-like species evolved. The praying mantises are the only modern survivors.

Scientists believe that the transition from cockroach to mantis happened in a series of steps rather than as one big change. A possible example of this is a 110-million-year-old praying mantis fossil found in Brazil in 2003. The fossil showed that an ancient species of praying mantis, named *Santanmantis axelrodi*, had a significant difference from modern species. Two sets of its legs have spines on them—unlike the modern species of praying mantis, which only have spines on the top forelegs. These spiny legs are what the insect uses to catch its prey. At some point in the evolution of the mantis, the second set of spines was lost.

MANTISES THAT LOOK LIKE A FLOWER

Female orchid mantises evolved in a way seen in no other arthropod: they look like orchids. Scientists examined praying mantis sizes, shapes, and DNA to figure out why. It seems they evolved to look that way to attract their flower-loving prey, such as bees and butterflies. Researchers believe that the ancestors of this mantis began waiting near orchids because they knew their flying food would soon make a visit. Then the females evolved to become larger in order to take advantage of the food opportunities. The bigger the female, the wider variety of prey she could hunt. Next, they developed their bright yellow, white, and pink colors to look similar to the flowers and confuse the pollinators. Meanwhile, males of the species are smaller and colored brown and green to blend in with the undergrowth and avoid predators. Scientists believe the males stayed small because they need to move around the environment to find females and mate.

CHAPTER FOUR

Beetles

Colorful beetles swarm the planet. There are more than 370,000 known species buzzing and scurrying pretty much everywhere on Earth except Antarctica.[1] They live in habitats ranging from snowy mountains to arid deserts. They are the largest order of insects, representing approximately 40 percent of insect species on the planet.[2] The smallest is the miniscule featherwing beetle, which can be smaller than 0.04 inches (1 mm).[3] The largest is the gigantic rhinoceros beetle at up to 6.7 inches (17 cm) long including its ferocious horn.[4]

Some beetles, such as ground beetles, scurry around on the damp ground, stalking their habitats for small insects and worms to munch. Leaf beetles make their territories among leaves and eat plants. They become pests when they chow down on cereal crops. Other groups of

Some beetles come in beautiful colors.

Fossils of insects, including those of beetles, are not as common as fossils of other types of animals, but they can provide valuable information on insect evolution.

beetles prefer an aquatic lifestyle. Diving beetles hunt their prey in fresh water, using their hind legs to swim.

EARLY BEETLES

The oldest known fossil of a beetle is from approximately 300 MYA. This means beetles were buzzing in the skies and lurking in the undergrowth even before the first dinosaurs appeared 245 MYA. Beetles then survived several extinctions, including the one that killed off dinosaurs 66 MYA.

The most successful groups of beetles eventually evolved into the thousands of species alive today. These beetle ancestors got their meals from flowering plants. Flowering plants are the most diverse group of plants and include apple trees, orchids, and grasses. This relationship between the evolution of beetles and flowering plants is an example of coevolution. Coevolution is when two species affect each other's evolution. In the case of flowering plants and beetles, some beetles evolved to feed on certain plants, and their feeding could kill the plant. The plants then evolved defenses against the beetles. This coevolution accounts for some of the exceptional diversity of both beetles and plants. It began when flowering plants started to grow

COEVOLUTION OF DUNG BEETLES AND DINOSAURS

Dung beetles roll dung into large balls. Dung beetles then feed on these balls and later lay their eggs in them, and the larvae also feed on the balls when they hatch. Scientists investigating the origin of dung beetles discovered they evolved approximately 130 to 115 MYA. Dinosaurs were alive at this time. Scientists compared the DNA of beetles that feed directly on plants to the DNA of dung beetles. It showed that both plant-eating beetles and dung beetles evolved alongside flowers. This is because dung beetles were feeding on the remains of those plants in the dinosaurs' dung. Fossilized dinosaur dung from 80 to 70 MYA has evidence of tunnels made by dung beetles as the beetles fed on the prehistoric creatures' waste. This supports the DNA evidence. The results of the DNA study also suggest the extinction of dinosaurs from 70 to 60 MYA stressed the dung beetle populations. But they survived. Scientists think that modern dung beetles could be descended from species that also fed on the dung of early mammals that were alive at the same time as dinosaurs.

Some beetle larvae live underground.

as long as 200 MYA. At the time, they were an untapped food source. The beetles that were able to evolve to feed on them enjoyed the new food source and continued to multiply. And as the beetles multiplied, the plants also diversified to evolve better defenses. Beetles evolved in response to the defenses.

Scientists determined this coevolution by examining the beetle and plant family trees. They looked at groups of close relatives to see which beetles had continued eating older, primitive plants such as pine trees and which beetles had begun to eat the newly evolved flowering plants. The beetles that switched to eating flowering plants were more diverse. While the evolution of flowering plants made beetles successful, beetles also owe some of their success to the evolution of full metamorphosis, elytra, and low levels of extinction early in their history.

METAMORPHOSIS

The earliest insects did not transform using metamorphosis. They hatched from eggs and looked like miniature forms of their parents. But between 300 and 280 MYA, some insects began to mature differently. They hatched looking nothing like their parents.

Wingless insects, such as silverfish, hatch from their eggs already looking like tiny versions of their parents. They grow larger over time by molting and shedding their exoskeletons. Insects such as cockroaches and dragonflies hatch as nymphs—smaller than their adult parents and with a few differences, such as a lack of wings. They gradually develop wings as they molt and grow. This process is incomplete metamorphosis. Beetles—as well as flies, butterflies, moths, and bees—hatch as larvae, then move into a pupal stage before finally emerging as adults. As many as 60 percent of all animal species on the planet today use metamorphosis.[5] It's a successful process because metamorphosis benefits both the offspring and the adult insects. Young and old insects don't compete for the same food. The larvae are happy munching on leaves and the adults reign over the skies and feed on nectar supplies.

Scientists combined evidence from the fossil record with studies on insect anatomy and development to try to understand how metamorphosis evolved. Complete metamorphosis likely evolved from incomplete metamorphosis. The oldest fossilized insects developed much like the modern insects that use incomplete metamorphosis. But fossils from 280 MYA show a different process—insects began to hatch from their eggs as creatures that looked like worms with legs. Scientists haven't been able to completely answer how insects evolved metamorphosis. But they have a theory. The nymphs of insects that don't use complete metamorphosis—such as dragonflies—go through a stage called the pronymphal stage while they're still in their eggs or when they're newly hatched. Scientists think this is equivalent to the larvae stage in beetles and the other insects that use full metamorphosis. So maybe at some point hundreds of millions of years ago, the pronymphal insects of beetles, butterflies, and moths started to hatch, feeding themselves with plants. Then they entered the pupal stage, the equivalent to the nymph stage of cockroaches and dragonflies, before becoming adults. Metamorphosis is just one of the beetle's evolutionary adaptations.

LIFE CYCLE OF A BEETLE

Adult beetles lay eggs in the best place for their offspring—in a plant, under a rock, in dung, or in tree trunks—depending on what the larvae will eat. Beetle larvae are wingless, and their job is to eat and grow. Eventually, when they've had their fill and grown in size, they enter the pupal stage. In this stage, the larva transforms into an adult using complete metamorphosis. Once the adult emerges from the pupa, its main job is to find a mate, produce eggs, and start the cycle all over again.

Beetles hold their elytra away from their bodies while in flight.

WINGS BECOME SHIELDS

Cockroaches evolved to have wings they could fold away, but beetles took it one step further. Beetles could injure their wings when they burrow under leaves on the ground to lay eggs or to hide. Fighting other males could also injure their wings. So beetles evolved hardened front wings that they fold back to protect their delicate flight wings and their bodies. These wing shields are called elytra. When it's time to take flight, these shields open, and their flight wings unfurl until they're stretched to their full size, ready to lift off.

Elytra are thought to be one of the main evolutionary innovations that led to so many species of beetles all over the planet. The elytra protect the beetles' wings and bodies from

Rhinoceros beetles are known for their prominent horns.

damage while the insects are wedged in tight spaces under rocks or bark. Elytra protect beetles from infection by microbes and fungi. They allow bugs to squeeze into warm hiding places without damaging their wings, so the creatures can survive freezing temperatures. The elytra can also help the beetle prevent water loss so it can survive in very dry conditions.

EVOLVING DEFENSES

In addition to elytra, male beetles have evolved methods to defend themselves against rival males. Male stag beetles have evolved large mandibles, or mouthparts, in a range of amazing shapes. Some of these weapons are as long as their own bodies, so the beetles have to contend with reduced running speed and stability as well as potential impaired flight performance. A 2015 study concluded that male stag beetles use 26 percent more power than females to fly with their heavy weapons but that the shape of the antlers didn't affect their flight. The size and shape of the mandible only had a tiny influence on flight performance (less than 0.1 percent).[6] The scientists concluded that the evolution of stag beetle weaponry is constrained by its excessive weight, not by the size or shape of the mandibles. Therefore, many different shapes and styles of antler-like weapons have evolved among beetles.

Some beetles have large horns. A 2007 study suggested that the size of horns can depend on the nutrition obtained by the beetle

BIOLUMINESCENCE

The firefly, a type of beetle, produces a chemical reaction inside its body that makes it glow. This is called bioluminescence. Fireflies glow to warn predators or to attract a mate. A theory on how fireflies got their light begins with the larvae. Instead of using vivid colors to warn away predators, which would be useless as they're active at night, their light evolved as a warning system. Over the course of millions of years, adult fireflies started to signal each other, this time using the light to attract a partner. Many other species of animals, such as angler fish, have also evolved to use light. Unlike the firefly's light, the angler fish's light is used to attract prey.

BEETLES THAT PRETEND TO BE ANTS

There are species of beetles that have evolved masterful disguises. Rove beetles have evolved to resemble army ants. They look, smell, and act like the ants, and they even go on hunting raids with ants. But when the army ants least expect it, the beetles turn on their unsuspecting housemates and eat their young.

in the larval stage. Poor nutrition leads to a small adult beetle with small wings and small horns. In 2014, scientist Erin McCullough discovered that horns evolved to have shapes that best suit each beetle species' fighting style. Male beetles with long horns tend to fence or wrestle. Males with curved horns tend to ram their opponents. Males with short, smooth horns are most likely to stab. The beetles who are most successful with their defenses then go on to breed, and their genes get passed down to their offspring.

Bombardier beetles, in the family Carabidae, have a method to defend themselves against predators. When a potential predator disturbs them, they eject a boiling toxic chemical spray. The spray is produced from a reaction between two chemical compounds: hydroquinone and hydrogen peroxide. The chemicals are stored in the beetle's abdomen. When the chemicals meet with a catalyst in a reaction chamber, the heat from the reaction produces gas. This gas causes the chemical to eject, injuring or at least frightening off the beetle's attacker. It makes the beetle invulnerable to most other animals. Bombardier beetles have even been known to escape the stomach of an attacker, such as a toad, using their explosive weapon.

Scientists aren't entirely sure how bombardier beetles evolved this amazing weapon. But they have noted possible evolutionary steps by studying the different species of bombardiers. Some have more-developed weapons than others. Some have a simple defense, such as formic acid. Others expel only a little toxic foam. But the African bombardier beetle has a sophisticated cannon that ejects more foam. This leads scientists to believe that hints about the foundations of the bombardier beetles' sophisticated spray might be seen throughout the family Carabidae.

EVOLUTION OF COLOR

Many beetles have evolved colorful, patterned elytra. There are two ideas about why this happened. One is that colorful elytra are a warning to predators not to eat them. Another is that the elytra provide camouflage. Scientists studying leaf beetles in Australia observed that some beetles had similar colors to the plants they lived on, suggesting it was an advantage for the beetles to evolve to be camouflaged by the plant, helping them evade predators. It is an example of natural selection because camouflage meant that these beetles couldn't be easily spotted by hungry predators. These camouflaged beetles survived and had offspring with the same camouflage.

Ladybugs come in many different colors, not just the red with black spots most people recognize. Some are orange, yellow, or even brown. These colors help protect ladybugs from predators in different ways. A study in the United Kingdom revealed that the color of the beetle tells predatory birds how toxic they are. The brighter the color, the more toxic the ladybug. Birds also understand that signal. The birds are less likely to feed on the most brightly colored ladybugs. Ladybugs with duller colors have lower levels of toxin. However, their colors make them more camouflaged against plants, keeping them hidden from predators. The more conspicuous and colorful species flaunt their strong defenses to deter birds from eating them.

Ladybugs come in several shades besides red, including orange.

Butterflies come in many colors and patterns.

CHAPTER FIVE

Butterflies and Moths

There are more than 18,000 known butterfly species and approximately 140,000 known moth species that make up the group Lepidoptera.[1] Some flutter around backyards. Others undertake enormous migrations. For example, monarch butterflies travel up to 3,000 miles (4,800 km) during winter from the northern parts of North America to warmer climates in California and Mexico.[2] And the rain forests of South America are filled with brightly colored butterflies such as the blue morpho, one of the largest butterflies in the world. Moths, usually nocturnal, are less colorful than butterflies. The adults of most species of moths and butterflies eat nectar from flowers. They suck the nectar with proboscises, which are

HOW DOES A CATERPILLAR TRANSFORM?

Caterpillars turn into butterflies and moths using complete metamorphosis, just like beetles. When the caterpillars have eaten their fill and have grown in size, they change into a pupa protected by a hard covering called a chrysalis. In moths, this covering is called a cocoon. As a pupa, the caterpillar transforms into a winged adult. To do this, the caterpillar releases enzymes to break down its tissues into proteins. People used to think the whole body broke down into something resembling a soup. But this isn't quite true—some organs stay intact. Other parts of the caterpillar, including muscles, break down into clumps of cells that can be reused. Other cells create structures called imaginal discs that produce adult body parts including the antennae, eyes, legs, and wings. Scientists know all this by dissecting pupae, but modern technology has led to a new way to view what happens when the insect is in the pupa stage. Scientists use a technique called micro-CT to scan the caterpillars as they change into butterflies within their chrysalises. Then the scientists combine the images into a three-dimensional (3-D) virtual model, showing the full process of metamorphosis.

long, tubelike mouthparts. After a meal, these proboscises curl away like tiny straws under their heads.

Like beetles, butterflies and moths undergo complete metamorphosis. These insects lay eggs. Wingless caterpillars hatch from these eggs and munch their way through leaves and plants to store up energy and to grow big enough for the next stage of their lives. But fat caterpillars can look pretty tasty to hungry birds and lizards. So caterpillars evolved many defense mechanisms. Some swallowtail butterfly caterpillars have a cunning disguise: they look like bird poop. No bird would want to gobble that. If a bird decided to give it a taste anyway, this caterpillar emits a nasty smell to send the bird flapping away. Other caterpillars

Caterpillars have a variety of traits that make them less appealing meals to potential predators.

are armed with spines to sting predators or bright colors to warn them off. The caterpillars of the skipper butterfly have an ingenious solution. They hide under leaf tents that they make themselves by chewing a suitably sized and shaped piece of leaf. They pull these tents over themselves while they munch their leafy dinners. The next stage of development is the pupa, in which the caterpillar wraps itself in a protective casing while turning into its adult form. The adults finally emerge, dry out their wings, and find a good spot to lay the eggs that will become the next generation of fluttering butterflies.

THE FIRST BUTTERFLIES AND MOTHS

Scientists believe that the earliest ancestors of butterflies and moths date back to approximately 250 MYA. But there are few fossils of butterflies and moths because their soft bodies and delicate wings don't preserve well. So scientists know little about those ancestors. The earliest

MOTHS KEEP THEIR CATERPILLAR MEMORIES

In metamorphosis, most of the caterpillar's tissues break down before reassembling to form a butterfly or moth. So it seems unlikely they would remember experiences from their caterpillar days. However, scientists have discovered that a moth keeps the memories it formed while it was a caterpillar. In an experiment, scientists taught caterpillars to avoid the smell of ethyl acetate (the chemical in nail polish remover) by giving them a mild electric shock when they encountered the smelly chemical. Seventy-eight percent of the caterpillars learned to avoid the odor in favor of fresh air. When the trained moths became adults a month later, 77 percent of them still avoided ethyl acetate.[3] So scientists know at least some part of caterpillars' memories survive to adulthood.

fossilized Lepidoptera wings are from the Jurassic period (201.3–145 MYA) and were found in Europe and central Asia. The oldest is from about 190 MYA from a species named *Archaeolepis mane*, and it was discovered in Dorset, England. Scientists analyzed the fossil with a powerful microscope and discovered that the scales and vein patterns on the wings were the same as on caddis flies. Caddis flies are related to the Lepidoptera group—they're known as a sister group. Caddis flies look like moths and live near freshwater habitats such as lakes and rivers. They're even attracted to light at night, just like their moth relatives. However, in one way, they're very different from the Lepidoptera group. Their larvae live in the water, whereas the caterpillars of moths and butterflies

Caddis flies live by rivers and lakes.

live on land. But scientists know they're closely related by studying their similar features, by analyzing their DNA for similarities, and by studying their fossils.

In 2014, researchers studying the DNA of butterflies published evidence showing that butterflies evolved from a particular group of small moths. The scientists proposed plume and geometrid moths as a sister group to butterflies.

Early Lepidoptera ancestors didn't have proboscises. Instead, they chewed their food with mandibles. One group of moths still does this today. Micropterigidae moths are usually small, fly during the day, and munch on pollen instead of sucking up nectar. As butterflies and moths evolved, adults lost their mandibles and developed a proboscis instead.

EVOLUTION OF THE PROBOSCIS

Modern butterflies and moths have a proboscis to help them suck up nectar from flowers. So for a long time, scientists presumed butterflies and moths evolved their proboscises because plants developed flowers. But a study has produced evidence suggesting that the feeding tubes evolved millions of years before flowers appeared. Scientists found fossilized butterfly scales from 200 MYA—approximately 70 million years older than the first flowers. The scales were so tiny the researchers had to use a human hair to push the scales onto a microscope slide to examine them. The scales were hollow, and only butterflies and moths with proboscises have hollow scales. Maybe there is a gap in the fossil record, and flowers evolved earlier than scientists thought. But for now, the scientists who examined the fossils think the evidence

COEVOLUTION WITH FLOWERING PLANTS

Like beetles, butterflies and moths coevolved with flowering plants. The insects feed on flowers' nectar. In return, the insects distribute the flowers' pollen, enabling the plants to reproduce and survive. An example is in the relationship between a Madagascan orchid and Darwin's moth. The orchid's nectar is hidden at the end of a tube one foot (30 cm) from the top of the flower.[4] Darwin's moth has evolved with a proboscis that is the same length. As it feeds, it gets the pollen from the orchid on its body, which it then transfers to another orchid, allowing the flower to reproduce.

suggests butterflies and moths evolved their proboscises before flowers. Maybe they used proboscises to drink sugary pollination drops that flowerless plants and trees, such as pine trees, produced at the time.

WING EVOLUTION

Butterflies have two pairs of wings, just like dragonflies, but they use them differently. They use them like one pair of wings—the larger front pair overlaps the smaller rear pair, making them beat as one. This means each wing beat can give them a huge amount of lift, so they don't need as many wing beats to stay airborne. It also means they can be agile in the air, making them harder for predators to catch.

Butterflies' wings are covered in tiny scales overlapping each other like roof shingles. Some of the scales contain pigment to give them their beautiful mosaic of colors. Other butterflies have scales that bend light to give them an iridescent sheen. Every species of butterfly has its own unique wing pattern, which helps males find females to mate with and identifies other males of the same species as rivals. Of course, these bright wings can also cause problems because hungry birds can spot them too. So butterflies tend to keep their wings closed on their backs when perched.

HUMMINGBIRDS AND HUMMINGBIRD MOTHS

Convergent evolution is when two species of unrelated animals evolve to have the same characteristics to solve the same problem. In the case of hummingbirds and hummingbird hawk moths (pictured), the problem was how to extract nectar from deep inside flowers. The hummingbird developed a long beak. The moth developed a long proboscis. But both hover at the flowers until they've consumed their fill of sweet nectar.

Butterflies and moths can also use their wings to confuse and defend against predators. Moths are nocturnal flyers. So their wings are used for camouflage while they rest during the day. They keep their wings open and blend into the bark or leaves they're resting on. Butterflies can display bright colors, such as the orange hues on a monarch butterfly, to warn predators they're poisonous—and some species do that even if they're not poisonous.

Other butterflies, such as the owl butterfly, have evolved large eyespots on the undersides of their wings so predators think they're much bigger than they are. Scientists don't agree on whether this owl mimicry is intentional. Some studies say the fake owl eyes make them more conspicuous and therefore more likely to get

Some eyespots protect butterflies from predators. Others help them find a mate.

eaten. Butterflies have a second line of defense—they can flash their more colorful upper-side patterns to confuse the predator and buy themselves a few seconds to escape. For example, the owl butterfly has contrasting blue and orange scales on the topside of its wings. One theory of the origin of eyespots is that they evolved from simpler, single spots. Another theory is that they evolved from a band of color on the wing, which later separated into spots. When the spots evolved in such a way that they became useful by confusing predators, the butterflies with the spots survived and the design was passed on to future generations of butterflies. In another species, the eyespots developed on the top side of the wings, but this time they had a different function: to attract a mate.

Flies can transmit diseases, but they can also play important roles in their ecosystems.

CHAPTER SIX

Flies and Fleas

Many people think of flies and fleas as pests, but there is a wide variety of fly and flea species. There are more than 125,000 known species of flies in the Diptera order today.[1] They account for approximately 10 percent of animal species on the planet.[2] Fleas are part of the Siphonaptera order, and there are approximately 2,500 different flea species.[3]

Unlike butterflies and dragonflies, flies only have a single pair of wings. A rear pair has evolved into halteres. These club-like organs tell the fly what its body position is in the air and help it undertake fast and tricky maneuvers to evade danger, such as a flyswatter or a predator. When fly eggs hatch, the larvae, called maggots, live in

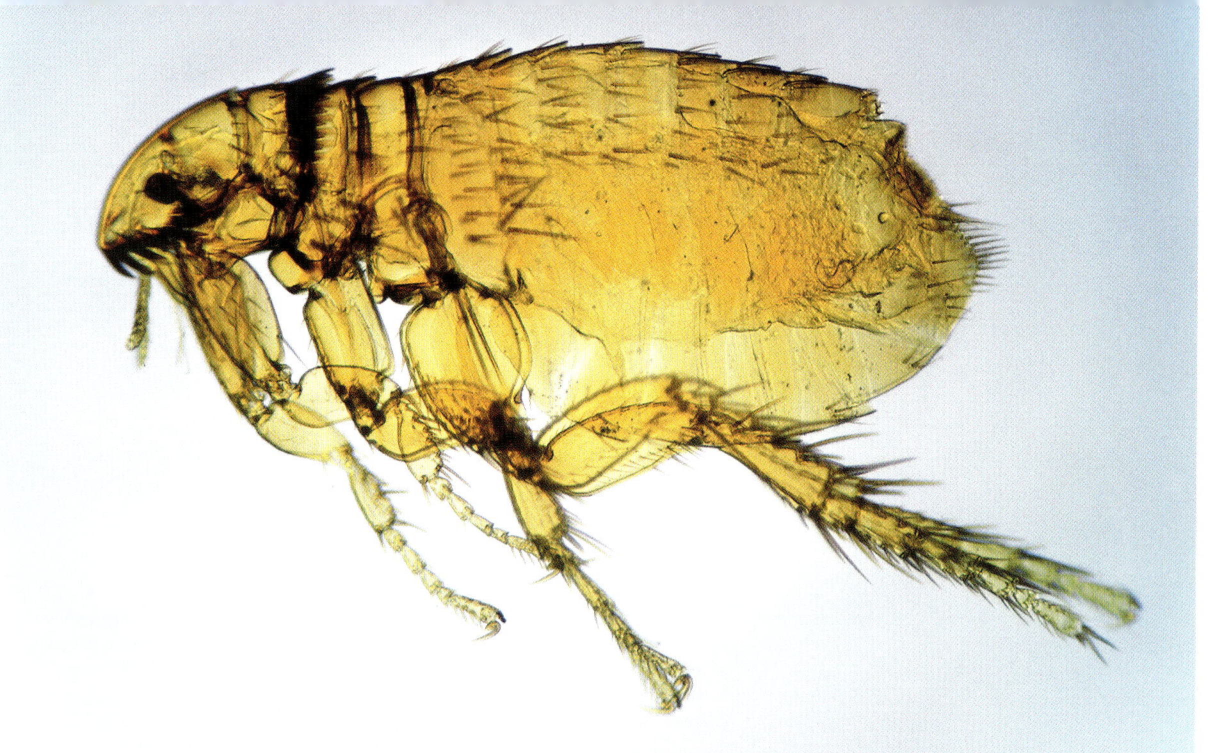

Fleas are very small. Scientists use strong magnification to take photos of them.

water, soil, bark, or even in pools of crude petroleum. Adults have mouthparts that have evolved to suck up juices from plants or animals. For example, mosquitoes feed on blood, and common houseflies feed on decomposing matter. Flies can spread dangerous diseases including malaria and typhoid.

Fleas have evolved to be flightless. They use their strong hind legs to jump from host to host—these champion high jumpers can leap distances 200 times their body length.[4] Once they find a suitable body to land on, they use their sharp, thin mouthparts to pierce the skin and suck up their host's blood.

EARLY FLIES

Flies have had three stages of exceptional diversification in their history: 220, 160, and 65 MYA. This means lots of new species appeared at each of those times. One of the oldest fly families still alive today is the mountain midges. These flies have long legs and long wings. Their larvae live in fast-flowing mountain water.

Another species of early flies was mosquitoes. Scientists believe early mosquitoes fed on plants or other insects. Then at some point in their history, a group of mosquitoes discovered the taste of blood and evolved to suck on animals. There are 3,500 known species of mosquito, but most of those feed on nectar. Only females from 6 percent of mosquito

FRUIT FLIES

Fruit flies share approximately 60 percent of human genes, so they're useful for research on human diseases such as cancer and diabetes.[5] Fruit flies eat—as their name suggests—fruit, and only have a life cycle of two weeks.[6] This makes them perfect for studying the mutation of genes, since a new generation is born every couple of weeks. Evolution occurs rapidly. Six Nobel prizes have been awarded to scientists who have used fruit flies to conduct groundbreaking research projects.[7] One prizewinning project focused on researching circadian rhythms—the internal clock that tells animals when to be awake and when to sleep. Scientists used fruit flies to figure out which genes controlled this mechanism and how it works.

UNDERGROUND MOSQUITOES

The London Underground has more than 1.3 billion people using its trains every day.[9] But they probably don't know that many animals call London's subway network home—including a species of mosquito that evolved in the unique conditions of the underground environment. The London Underground mosquito was first reported during World War II (1939–1945), when the subway tunnels were used as bomb shelters. Aboveground relatives of these mosquitoes feed on birds, but birds don't live in the tunnels. These mosquitoes evolved to feast on human blood instead. Scientists think this evolution occurred over just a few hundred generations, in the time since the underground system was constructed.

species suck blood from humans.[8] But they're now considered one of the most dangerous animals in the world because they spread deadly diseases such as malaria and the Zika virus.

Scientists believe mosquitoes' relatives originated approximately 226 MYA. However, the oldest fossil is from 100 to 90 MYA. This amber fossil found in Burma contains a species related to modern mosquitoes. In the 1980s, a fossil from 46 MYA was unearthed in Montana. The insect still contained blood in its stomach, showing that the insects had started feeding on other animals by then.

Like all organisms, flies are still evolving today. People spray their homes and farmers spray their crops with pesticides, chemicals meant to kill pests. But the use of pesticides has

Modern pesticides are prompting flies to adapt in order to survive.

led some species of flies to evolve resistance to these chemicals, thanks to natural selection. Every time chemicals are sprayed on crops to kill flies, a few naturally resistant insects survive. They then breed, and their offspring are also resistant to the chemicals. That generation breeds another even more resistant generation. Eventually, the pesticides no longer work.

EARLY FLEAS

The oldest fleas were five to ten times larger than today's fleas. They had sharp, sawlike teeth, but they lacked the strong hind legs of their modern descendants. Scientists discovered these giant fleas in fossils in China. The fossils date from 165 to 125 MYA, and the fleas were up to 0.8 inches (2 cm) long. In comparison, the fleas infesting mammals today are 0.1 inches (2.5 mm) long. Scientists think these ancient fleas might have fed on feathered dinosaurs rather than on the small mammals that were also scurrying around at the time.[10] The first fleas evolved from fly ancestors that fed on plant fluids. They evolved from feeding on plants to feeding on animal blood. The fleas lost their wings and developed legs that could cling to fur and feathers, allowing them to suck the blood of an unwitting host.

In 2012, a fossil from 125 MYA was found in China. Scientists believe it could be a transitional fossil that represents the change between the giant fleas and their modern descendants.

Flea bites cause skin irritation.

It was smaller than the older fossil, measuring 0.4 inches (1 cm) long, and had a relatively small sucking tube for drawing blood.[11] It was also missing the teeth of its older relative. This discovery suggests that fleas coevolved with their hosts. Mammals have thinner, more sensitive skin than dinosaurs. If the flea still had sharp teeth and was large, it would be more likely to be detected and swatted away. So the ability to take small sips of mammal blood and be agile enough to evade danger became more important than being large.

CHAPTER SEVEN

Bees, Wasps, and Ants

Bees, wasps, and ants are all members of the Hymenoptera order of insects. There are nearly 150,000 known living species in the order, including honey bees, yellow jackets, and leaf-cutter ants.[1]

Some members of the order are pollinators. Bumblebees release pollen from flowers by shaking them—the buzzing sound that fills the air in summer is created by the bees' vibrating. They feed their young the nutritious pollen, while the adult bees eat nectar. As the bees visit multiple flowers, they carry pollen with them, pollinating the plants. They pollinate many of the crops that humans rely on for food, including pumpkins, peaches, and peppers. Other members

Wasps are often predators, but they may also feed on nectar.

of Hymenoptera are predators. Hunting wasps take down arachnids as large as tarantulas to feed their offspring. Some wasps are parasitoids. They lay their eggs inside other insects, which their larvae then eat from inside, eventually killing the unwilling host. Some species of ants are predators, too. A colony of army ants will make a meal of other creatures including insects, reptiles, and even small mammals by swarming and consuming them.

Within Hymenoptera there have been several important evolutionary changes. Some species have evolved from eating wood to being parasitoids and predators. Others have evolved in the reverse direction. Some live and work in social groups, and some work alone.

EARLY ANCESTORS

The Hymenoptera order is one of the largest orders of insects on the planet today. They started life before dinosaurs roamed and birds flew. The earliest fossil ancestors of wasps, bees, and ants have been found in Australia, Asia, and Africa. These early ancestors were ancient sawflies from approximately 235 MYA. Scientists knew the fossils were sawflies because of the distinctive vein pattern on their wings that members of this group all share. Sawflies look like wasps and get their name from the sawlike appearance of the ovipositor—the tube females use to lay eggs. The sawfly uses the ovipositor to cut into leaves and make a safe space for her offspring

Large numbers of ants can quickly consume large prey.

to hatch. Sawflies feed on plants and trees such as pines and ferns, making them a pest for gardeners. They live in most parts of the world.

WASPS

Wasps first appeared in the Jurassic. Unlike their wood-eating sawfly ancestors, wasps evolved to eat other insects. The development of two key features enabled this change of behavior. In wasps, the ovipositor has another function in addition to laying eggs. It evolved a stinger used

Some wasps lay their eggs on other insects. The larvae will then feed on the host insect.

to paralyze prey and to defend against predators. Another key to the success of wasps was the evolution of a wasp waist, a feature sawflies don't have. The waist was formed between the wasps' first and second abdominal segments. It greatly improved the wasps' ability to move the rear section of the abdomen. This is where the ovipositor, the stinger, is located. This new improved maneuverability may have led to the species' success as a predator.

An example of a wasp putting these adaptations to use is a parasitoid species of wasp, *Hymenoepimecis argyraphaga*, which uses an orb weaver spider as its host. The female wasp uses its ovipositor to sting and paralyze the spider, then she lays an egg on it. The larva develops and attaches to the spider, sucking fluid from the spider. After a few weeks, it's time to make a cocoon. But the larva needs a place to hang the cocoon. So the larva injects a chemical into its unwitting host, forcing the spider to spin a sturdy web for the baby wasp. Once the web is completed, the larva kills the spider and makes its cocoon on the web. A few weeks later, it emerges as a fully formed adult wasp. Other wasp families build nests and feed their larvae prey, like caterpillars and other insect larvae, directly. This is the group of wasps that bees evolved from.

THE FIRST BEES

Scientists believe the first bees evolved from wasps approximately 120 MYA. An amber fossil from 100 MYA contains a bee that looks like a wasp, supporting the idea that bees evolved

FIG TREE AND FIG WASPS

Fig wasps and fig trees are mutually dependent. Fig trees are dependent on the wasp to be pollinated. The wasp depends on the fig tree to produce its offspring. Female fig wasps have evolved to have the perfect shape that enables them to crawl into figs. The wasps bring with them pollen from another fig tree and pollinate the flowers, which grow inside the fruit, before laying their eggs inside. After the queen has laid her eggs, she dies and is absorbed by the fig. Once the eggs hatch, the male and female wasps mate with each other. Then the females collect pollen while the males begin cutting a path to the outside. The males don't leave the fig, however, since they don't have wings to fly anywhere. The females with their pollen leave through the tunnel the males have made and head off to pollinate other figs and lay their eggs inside. Scientists believe this mutually beneficial relationship first evolved approximately 60 MYA.

THE ORCHID AND ORCHID BEE

Orchids depend on orchid bees to pollinate them so they can reproduce. Orchids don't produce nectar, so most pollinators aren't interested in them. But the orchid bee comes to the flower for its fragrance. The bee uses this fragrance to attract a mate. Scientists once believed that orchids and orchid bees had coevolved by changing a little bit, in turn, over time. But new evidence suggests that the orchid needs the bees more than the bees need the flower. The bees get their special fragrance from other plant species and fungi as well as the orchid. But the orchid depends on the orchid bee for pollination. Other bees don't visit it because it doesn't have nectar. As the bees evolve new preferences for the compounds they use as fragrance, the orchids evolve new compounds, so the orchid bees keep returning.

from wasps around the same time that flowers started to appear on the planet. The fossilized bee even had tiny pollen grains attached to its body.

Despite their wasp ancestors being predators, bees eat pollen. A theory for this change in diet is that the predatory wasps started bringing pollen for their young to eat, and eventually a group developed that only ate pollen. This group diversified and became bees. There are 2,200 species of hunting wasps but more than 20,000 described species of bees, so this change from predation to eating pollen appears to have been a significant reason for bees' success.[2] "The switch from predatory behavior in hunting wasps to pollen feeding in bees has led to a tenfold increase in

Some wasps hunt prey larger than themselves.

diversification. Our findings support the idea that the switch to a vegetarian lifestyle in bees is a really big deal in terms of explaining bee diversity on earth," said Bryan Danforth, professor of entomology, who studied the DNA of bees, wasps, and ants to figure out how they're related.[3] Danforth's DNA study confirmed the fossil evidence that bees and ants evolved from wasps. Danforth and his team looked for DNA sequences that were similar or identical across species to determine the evolutionary relationships among the groups of ants, wasps, and bees.

Bees gather around another bee as it shows them where to find nectar.

Like termites and ants, honeybees live in social groups. However, they have evolved a unique technique among insects. They can tell their fellow bees where to find nectar by performing what is called a waggle dance. The angle the bee dances in tells the other bees which direction to fly in, relative to the direction of the sun. And the length of the moves along the honeycomb tells them how far to go. Scientists believe the use of the waggle dance evolved approximately 20 MYA. One explanation for why the dance originally evolved was so the honeybees could find suitable nesting sites. Later it became a way of locating food. When bee colonies look for a new nest site, they send out scouting bees who then communicate the new location with a dance. When enough scouts have determined that a location is a good nest site, the whole swarm moves to the new location.

ANTS

The oldest true ants first appeared in the fossil record approximately 100 MYA, and scientists studying their DNA believe they evolved from a species of wasp called mud daubers. Scientists have discovered ants in amber found in France, Canada, and Burma. These ants didn't look like the kind that scurry around backyards and infest kitchens—they had whiskers and long hairs on their heads. Their strong jaws helped them devour their prey. Ant species feed on a variety of different foods, including nectar, seeds, fungi, and other animals. At some point in their evolution, most ants lost their wings. They hunted all their prey on the ground, so ants had no need for wings.

Ants live just about everywhere on the planet except Antarctica. One estimate says there are 10,000 trillion ants on Earth right now.[4] Scientists studying ants in a Brazilian rain forest discovered the total mass of ants that called the forest home was approximately four times greater than the combined mass of all the mammals, reptiles, and amphibians in the forest.

FUNGUS FARMERS

Ants in a South American rain forest farm fungus underground. They tend their tiny crops, even weeding and watering them. Scientists studying their DNA believe they first started farming approximately 60 MYA. Thirty million years later, the fungus farmers split into two groups. One group evolved to grow its fungus in dry desert areas, and the fungus evolved to be completely dependent on its ant farmers because it couldn't grow freely in the environment. The ant famers control the temperatures of their minifarms by digging deeper chambers. They maintain humidity by bringing in water from fruits, plants, or morning dew. The other group stayed in the wet rain forests where the fungus is more likely to grow elsewhere beyond the tiny farms. Today, around 250 different species of ants build their own farms and harvest fungus for food.[5] The ants remove any bad fungi that threaten the rest of the crop.

Social groups provide many benefits that may be responsible for how populous ants are in many habitats.

Ants live in large colonies where they divide up the jobs. Some find food, others rear the young, and others are in charge of defending the nests. There is an evolutionary advantage to living in groups like this. As a group, they can defend their nest and work together to find food.

The ant's ancestors, the mud dauber wasps, create mud cylinders in which to lay their eggs. Scientists think this behavior might be what led to ants forming social groups. Ant ancestors may have started by building simple nests and bringing food to their larvae. Then they may

Mud dauber wasps sometimes build their nests along the walls of buildings.

have started bringing multiple smaller meals to multiple larvae. Then those offspring grew up and started doing the same thing.

In such a large system of insects, it might be presumed that individuals would be unimportant and easily replaced. But a species of ant in Africa, *Megaponera analis,* has been observed carrying wounded ants back to the colony. The wounded soldiers are needed for future raids on their food source, termites, and are soon back in action. Scientists believe there are several factors that made the behavior evolve. These ants hunt in groups. They have a high injury rate thanks to the termites fighting back. And they live in small colonies, making each individual important.

CHAPTER EIGHT

Grasshoppers, Crickets, and Katydids

The Orthoptera order of insects is a huge and diverse group of winged insects including grasshoppers, crickets, and katydids. There are more than 25,000 different species in the order.[1] They live all over the world, from backyards to rain forests. Crickets vary in length from 0.12 to 2 inches (3 to 50 mm) and have modified hind legs that help them jump to evade predators and find mates.[2] Katydids are larger and grow up to more than 2.4 inches (6 cm) long.[3] They can't fly very well and rely on camouflage to hide from predators. They look like the leaves of

Katydids are mainly nocturnal, though some species are active during the day.

flowering plants so they can blend in and hide. Grasshoppers are even bigger at up to 4.3 inches (11 cm) long.[4] They have strong hind legs for jumping and tend to be green or brown to hide in the undergrowth.

ORIGINS OF ORTHOPTERA

A study published in 2015 helped scientists figure out the origins of orthopterans. Before this study, scientists based their conclusions about the relationships between grasshoppers, crickets, and katydids on the way they looked. But organisms can have similar physical features despite not being closely related. Looking at the DNA sequences for the insects is more accurate.

Using DNA sequences, the researchers concluded that the Orthoptera order originated between 350 and 300 MYA, making it one of the oldest groups of insects. That order has diverged into two groups: Ensifera and Caelifera. Katydids and crickets are in the Ensifera group. Grasshoppers are in the Caelifera group.

The researchers concluded that crickets first evolved from individuals in the Ensifera group approximately 250 to 200 MYA and continued to evolve during the time of dinosaurs in the Jurassic. Katydids appeared next, evolving from individuals in the Ensifera group 145 to 65 MYA. The rise of katydids coincided with the rise of flowers. Flowers are an important

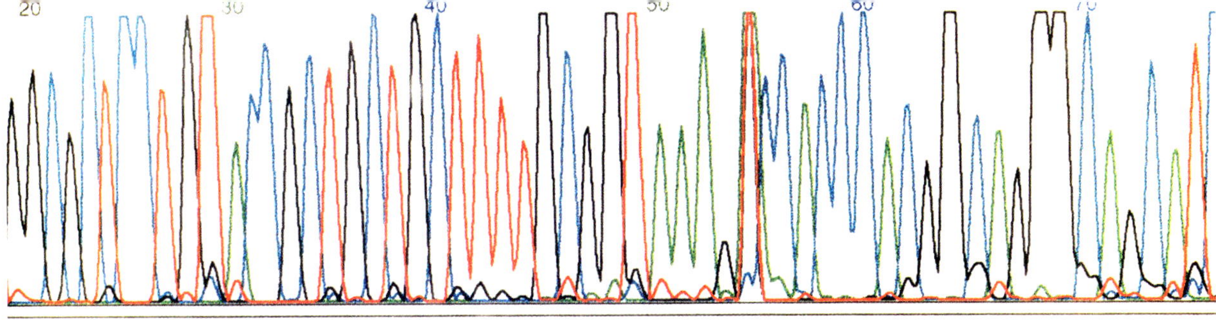

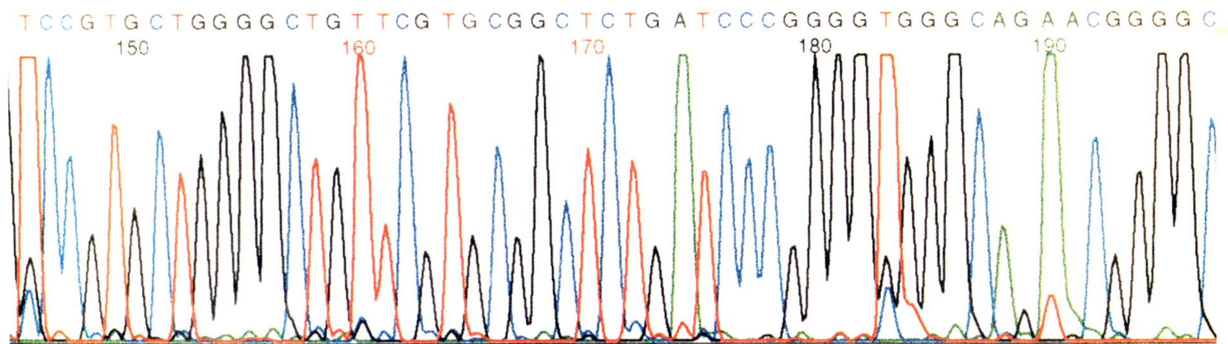

Scientists use computers to quickly detect patterns in DNA sequences.

part of the katydids' strategy to hide from predators because flowers can provide camouflage against predators.

Finally, the grasshoppers started evolving from the Caelifera group approximately 65 MYA. Their evolution coincided with the increase in grasslands. As their name suggests, grasshoppers are herbivores and rely on a steady diet of grass.

INSECT SONG

Grasshoppers usually jump from stem to stem, chewing plants with their strong scissor-shaped mandibles. Their powerful hind legs can propel them to distances 20 times their own length.

The ridges along a grasshopper's large hind legs help it make its song.

That's like a six-foot (1.8 m) person jumping 120 feet (37 m).[5] Grasshoppers have two sets of wings. The front set are leathery and used to protect the hind wings. As well as using wings to fly and evade predators, many grasshoppers have another use for their wings—music. A vein on the front pair of wings acts like a violin string as the grasshopper rubs its legs, which have several pegs on them, along the vein. It's mostly the male grasshoppers that make the buzzing song to attract a female. Every grasshopper species has its own unique sound.

Crickets also sing. The male crickets use their wings to create music by rubbing them together—the wings have a scraper on one wing and teeth like a saw on the other that produce a chirp when rubbed together. Crickets usually save their singing for after dark. Then the sound of the males fills the air on summer nights. One species of cricket, the mole cricket, has a unique way of making itself heard. It lives underground. When it's time to mate, the male enters a special underground chamber to start making his music. There the sound carries and amplifies along passages that act like speakers to attract a female. The sound can be heard up to 0.5 miles (0.8 km) away.[6]

In order to hear these songs, grasshoppers, crickets, and katydids first needed ears. Insect

SILENT CRICKETS

On the Hawaiian island of Kauai, the crickets have gone silent. Why? To avoid being consumed by the parasitic maggots of the species *Ormia ochracea*, a kind of fly. The maggots' parents follow a cricket's chirps and lay their offspring on the cricket's back. Maggots hatch from the eggs and then burrow into the cricket to feed on it. A week later they emerge, killing their host. But in an example of rapid evolution—just a few years—crickets on the island have gone silent so the flies can't find them.[7]

Scientists think a single gene mutation to change the shape of the male crickets' wings is what has made them silent—turning their wings into a similar shape to the silent females of the species. This means they can't chirp to attract a mate. But it seems the female crickets on the island have also evolved to not be so choosy and will settle for a silent mate. Scientists believe this may be because the silent males have also evolved to roam more, looking for a mate.

ears look very different from mammal ears. Crickets and katydids have tiny oval ears under their knees to detect predators. Scientists believed that the reason those ears evolved was to avoid newly evolved predators. But 50-million-year-old cricket and katydid fossils revealed that these ears evolved before the appearance of predators such as bats.

There is one other use for these insect ears. They detect mating calls, which helps insects find a partner to produce the next generation of insects. Because of the fossil evidence, scientists speculate that the original ears helped insects detect mating calls and only later evolved to detect predators. They are still researching to find the answer.

17-YEAR CICADAS

Cicadas chirping is a common sound in the summer, but some species of this singing insect are silent underground for years. The periodical cicadas—the longest-living insects in North America—emerge from their underground homes between May and June every 13 or 17 years.[8] The cicada larvae hatch and grow underground and live off sap from tree roots. The emergence of these insects is coordinated across multiple states, with billions of cicadas hitting the skies at the same time. Scientists think this synchronized emergence helps ensure the survival of the species—although large numbers of them will be eaten by predators, there are so many that enough will survive long enough to mate and lay more eggs.

EVOLUTION OF CAMOUFLAGE

In addition to leaping or flying away from predators, insects in order Orthoptera can use camouflage to avoid being eaten. In an example of natural selection, the insects have evolved characteristics that help them blend in with their habitats. They probably started developing these disguises around 126 MYA when the first insect predators also evolved, such as early birds and mammals.

Wings of katydids have evolved to blend in with the plants they call home. Katydids that look like leaves are less likely to get eaten, which means they survive and produce more young that look like leaves. This is an example of natural selection. One species of katydid evolved to look like lichen on trees, and it also eats the lichen. The katydid evolved to perfectly fit its habitat.

CRICKETS FOR LUNCH?

In 2014, the first edible-insects farm opened in the United States. Selling cricket chips, the store encouraged more people to try eating the chirping insects. Crickets are a more sustainable food than meat from mammals. A United Nations report released in 2013 showed that insects can provide protein more efficiently than cows, and raising the crickets emits only a fraction of the greenhouse gases released by cattle. Two billion people worldwide include insects as part of their diet.[9]

Scientists can learn some information about insects from fossils, but new technologies can help confirm theories and suggest new ones.

CHAPTER NINE

Research Today

The first scientists to describe natural selection and evolution were Charles Darwin and Alfred Russel Wallace. Wallace and Darwin spent their childhoods studying the natural world, especially beetles and their endless diversity of traits. Darwin eventually undertook a voyage to the Galápagos Islands. There, he studied animals and developed his theories, resulting in one of the most well-known books in the history of science—*On the Origin of Species*, published in 1859.

People have been digging up fossils for a long time, but fossils can only tell researchers so much. The fossil record is sparse, insects don't always preserve very well, and they can be hard to interpret. Modern techniques help overcome some of these hurdles.

CT SCANNING OF FOSSILS

Computed tomography (CT) scanners and X-ray machines are used by doctors to detect cancer or broken bones. But scientists can also use them to see inside rocks and opaque amber without having to break them open. The scientists use a much stronger form of radiation than would be safe for humans so they can penetrate the hard rock. This technology has been used for a while to study fossils. In 2009, scientists at the European Synchrotron Radiation Facility (ESRF)—a massive particle accelerator that creates intense beams of X-rays—scanned 100-million-year-old opaque amber and discovered a perfect wasp fossilized inside. If they'd had to break it open, the fossil would have been destroyed. Instead, they used a 3-D printer to create a plastic model so scientists could examine the creature in detail. They've scanned hundreds of fossils this way.

Researchers in Manchester, United Kingdom, have used the same technique to study fossils from 305 MYA. By using the scanner, the scientists can take 3,000 X-rays from different angles to accurately reproduce what tiny prehistoric animals looked like.[1] These scans help the researchers figure out clues to the lifestyle, biology, and diet of the insects. One of the cockroach-like insects

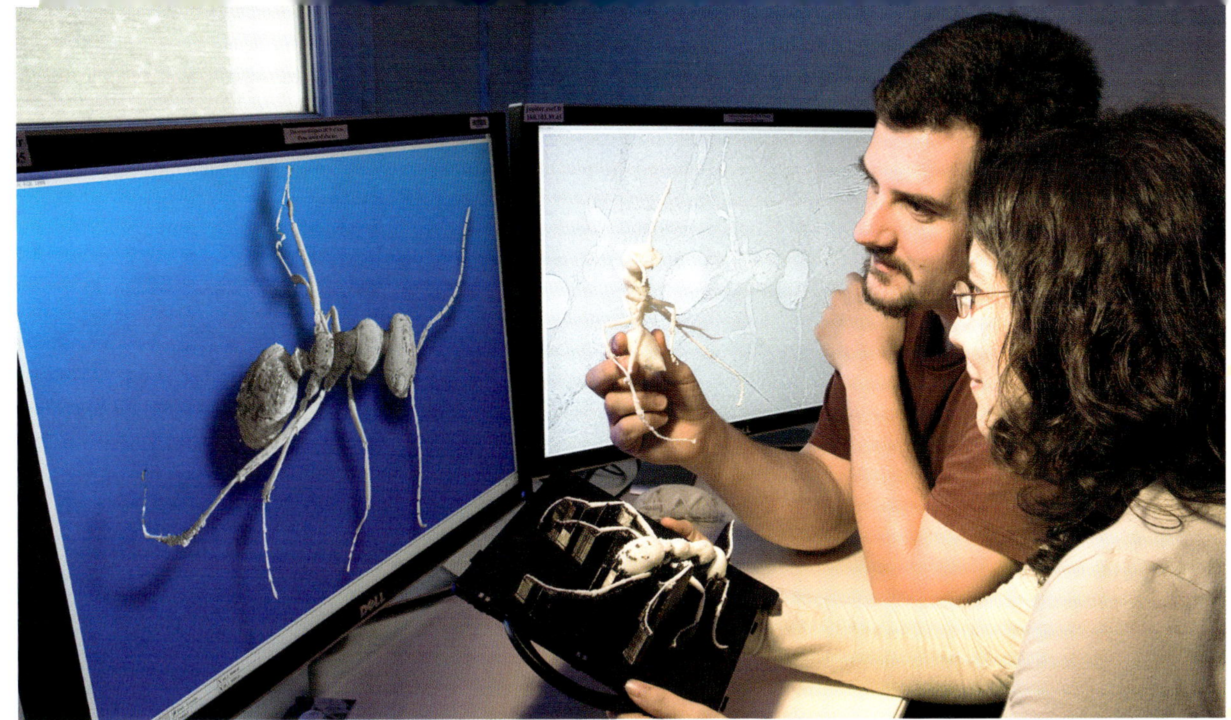

Scientists can make both digital and physical 3-D models of fossils.

they reconstructed had a large number of sharp spines—it was a new species that hadn't been seen before and that no longer exists.

INSECT TREE OF LIFE

One hundred experts in molecular biology, insect morphology, paleontology, insect taxonomy, evolution, and computing joined together to map the insect tree of life. They published their project in 2014. The group discovered the oldest ancestor of insects (the cave-dwelling remipedes) and concluded that insect flight likely started approximately 400 MYA, with dragonfly ancestors being some of the first to fly. They also mapped the relationships between insect groups. For example, they confirmed that mayflies and dragonflies are related and most likely evolved from the same ancestor. But they need to do more research to figure out how flies are related to them.

It was the first time such a gigantic project had been attempted. The researchers used data from 144 different species and calculated estimates on the dates of origin and the relationships for all the major insect groups.[2] One of the main hurdles the researchers had to overcome was how to deal with such a huge amount of information. They had to develop new software to process the data and construct the insect family tree.

METAL JAWS

Some insects have a surprising secret weapon in their jaws: metal. A fossil discovered in 2016 was found to contain zinc-lined mandibles. Scientists knew that some insects had metal in their mouths, but this was the first time it had been seen in a fossil. Scientists don't know when or why this surprising trait evolved, but they plan to investigate modern insects to see whether they have the same metallic features.

COCKROACH SECRETS

Scientists have assembled the American cockroach's genome—this means they've identified all the genes that make up the instructions that tell the cockroach's cells how to develop. It is the second-largest insect genome ever assembled, and it's larger than the human genome. The researchers discovered that the American cockroach has a large number of genes that control sensory perception, detoxification, the immune system, growth, and reproduction. This means that it's able to survive some pretty nasty conditions. It will live for a week with no head. It can even regrow a leg after it loses one. It will eat anything from poop to dead relatives. This research could help scientists figure out better pest-control methods. They might also gain insight into how the insect regrows limbs. If scientists can discover which genes control this process, it could have massive benefits for medicine.

Researchers have also studied the black blowfly. Black blowflies have a blue or green sheen and look similar to houseflies.

STUDYING LEAVES

Leaf fossils show insect bite marks, helping scientists determine which insects were flying and scuttling on the planet at certain times in its history. Ancient beetles, moths, flies, wasps, and grasshoppers all ate in unique ways, leaving behind damaged leaves that later became fossils. Some bit holes, some chewed along the veins, and others pierced the leaves to suck up juices. Larvae left behind tunnels, and eggs left behind lumps. Approximately 66 MYA, an asteroid wiped out the dinosaurs and 75 percent of animals and plants.[3] It took around nine million years for the insects in North America to recover, and these leaf fossils help scientists figure out which insects recovered first and where they lived. A surprising fact they uncovered was that insects in Patagonia recovered almost twice as fast as those in North America. Scientists don't yet know why the South American populations recovered faster.

Eyes

Insects use their compound eyes to process visual information approximately ten times faster than humans. Compound eyes are made up of many repeating units, each with its own lens and light receptor cells. The information from each unit gets combined into one single image—a bit like how pixels make up a digital photo. The more pixels in the image, the sharper it is. Compound eyes are the most obvious insect eyes, but insects can have other eyes as well. Some have both compound and ocelli eyes or just ocelli eyes.

Ocelli eyes have a single lens and can detect light. They do not give the insect a visual picture of its surroundings, but when an insect is flying, ocelli eyes can tell the insect where up (generally lighter) and down (generally darker) are. This form of eye can also help flies avoid predators, which would make the flies' vision darker as they approach.

Ancient arthropods lived in the ocean, where there was little color and where many animals were blind. But after the Cambrian explosion, animals diversified, and so did their eyes. Some of the earliest examples of compound eyes have been found in fossils from more than 500 MYA. Scientists believe the evolution of eyes gave creatures a huge advantage. They could navigate, find food, and avoid predators.

Scientists have discovered the gene they believe controls the growth of eyes. When a certain gene was activated by researchers in a fruit fly's legs or wings, the fly grew extra eyes on its legs or wings. This same gene is present in the simplest of multicellular animals, so scientists believe that all eyes evolved from simple eyes into the many complex eyes that animals such as humans, squids, and insects have today.

OCELLI EYES
COMPOUND EYES

Researchers in Indiana mapped the black blowfly's genome and believe they can use the results to figure out how the insect secretes and uses antimicrobial compounds. This could help them learn how to stop diseases in humans. This genome is also useful for researchers studying different insects that have unusual or dangerous characteristics, such as a species of fly that fatally attacks livestock. Scientists can compare the genome to others to see what the differences are and, therefore, which genes cause which behaviors.

LABORATORY-REARED INSECTS

Scientists can raise insects in their laboratories to conduct experiments and observe evolution—a process that would be difficult or impossible in nature. Lab-reared insects, such as mosquitoes, seem to thrive in the carefully monitored lab conditions. And thanks to those conditions, they have made several adaptations. They can evolve to produce more eggs that develop more quickly. The insects grow slightly larger and develop faster than their wild cousins. In labs, scientists can use these insects to study things like the spread of diseases and how to potentially halt them. For example, some scientists create lab-reared mosquitoes infected with bacteria and then release them into the wild. The lab-reared insects spread the bacteria to wild mosquitoes and may help halt the spread of diseases like the Zika virus.

Mosquitoes and other insects are useful for studying evolution because of their short life cycles.

Some of the other insects reared in artificial conditions include parasitoid wasps that are bred and then released to attack farm pests and therefore reduce the use of pesticides on crops. Scientists need to ensure that these wasps will survive in the wild after they've lived in controlled laboratory conditions.

Insects' long and complex evolutionary history is still being unraveled. Scientists studying insects and their evolution keep researching and describing new fossils, new family members, and new discoveries. Sometimes they discover something that contradicts evidence another scientist discovered. Other times they confirm what had previously been presumed. The story of insect evolution is still being written by scientists on the cutting edge of this research today.

ESSENTIAL FACTS

PERIOD TIMELINE

CAMBRIAN	ORDOVICIAN	SILURIAN	DEVONIAN	CARBONIFEROUS	PERMIAN
541–485.4 million years ago (MYA)	485.4–443.8 MYA	443.8–419.2 MYA	419.2–358.9 MYA	358.9–298.9 MYA	298.9–251.9 MYA
			Rhyniognatha hirsti bristletails	ancestors of grasshoppers and crickets	

NUMBER OF SPECIES

There are more than one million known insect species on the planet.

IMPORTANT ANIMALS AND SPECIMENS

- *Rhyniognatha hirsti* from 400 MYA is the oldest known insect fossil.
- Among the first insects were bristletails—fossils have been found from more than 390 MYA.
- Some of the oldest insects include the ancestors of grasshoppers and crickets that evolved around 350–300 MYA.
- *Archaeolepis mane* from 190 MYA is the oldest known Lepidoptera specimen with fossilized wings.
- *Santanmantis axelrodi* was a mantis that lived 110 MYA and had several differences from modern mantises.

ancient sawflies	*Archaeolepis mane*	*Santanmantis axelrodi*			
251.9–201.3 MYA	201.3–145 MYA	145–66 MYA	66–23 MYA	23–2.6 MYA	2.6 MYA–present
TRIASSIC	JURASSIC	CRETACEOUS	PALEOGENE	NEOGENE	QUATERNARY

IMPORTANT SCIENTISTS

- Charles Darwin and Alfred Russel Wallace independently published the first accurate descriptions of evolution.
- Coby Schal developed a theory on how modern cockroaches evolved to avoid glucose.
- David Grimaldi and Michael Engel wrote a book published in 2005, *Evolution of the Insects*. They also described the oldest insect fossil ever found, *Rhyniognatha hirsti*.
- Erin McCullough discovered that beetle horns evolved to suit their flying styles.

QUOTE

"The switch from predatory behavior in hunting wasps to pollen feeding in bees has led to a tenfold increase in diversification. Our findings support the idea that the switch to a vegetarian lifestyle in bees is a really big deal in terms of explaining bee diversity on earth."

—Bryan Danforth, entomologist

GLOSSARY

algae
Plantlike organisms that mostly grow in water and are often green, blue, red, or brown colored.

catalyst
A substance that increases the rate of chemical reactions without undergoing any changes itself.

crustacean
A typically aquatic invertebrate with an exoskeleton and two pairs of antennae; includes crabs, barnacles, and shrimp.

DNA
Deoxyribonucleic acid, the chemical that is the basis of genetics, through which various traits are passed from parent to child.

elytra
The hardened front wings that act like shields for beetles' hind wings.

entomologist
A scientist who studies insects.

eurypterid
An animal belonging to an extinct order of arthropods also known as sea scorpions.

gene
A unit of hereditary information found in a chromosome.

iridescent
Having the appearance of changing color as the viewing angle changes, such as on a soap bubble.

larva
An immature form of an animal that changes its body form through metamorphosis.

lobe
A body part that is rounded.

microbe
A microscopic living thing.

natural selection
The major mechanism by which evolution occurs. A trait that offers an advantage for organisms in a population will become more common because those organisms will live longer and produce more offspring.

nymph
A young insect that appears similar to the adult stage, such as in dragonflies and grasshoppers; a stage in incomplete metamorphosis.

parasitoid
An insect, often a wasp, that uses another insect to grow its young. When the new adult wasp emerges from its host, this kills the host.

pollinate
To transfer pollen from one flower to another in order to reproduce.

pupa
The dormant stage of metamorphosis when the insect changes from larval form into adult form.

sediment
Stones and sand that settle and form a layer; when sediment builds up over thousands of years it can form rock.

sister group
The closest living relative of a group of organisms.

soft tissue
Fat, skin, muscle, and other soft parts of the body that connect and support organs and bones.

thorax
The middle of the three main divisions of the body of an insect; the other two divisions are the head and abdomen.

ADDITIONAL RESOURCES

SELECTED BIBLIOGRAPHY

Attenborough, David. *Life in the Undergrowth*. Princeton UP, 2005.

Grimaldi, David, and Michael S. Engel. *Evolution of the Insects*. Cambridge UP, 2005.

Shaw, Scott R. *Planet of the Bugs: Evolution and the Rise of Insects*. U of Chicago, 2014.

FURTHER READINGS

Amstutz, Lisa J. *Invasive Species*. Abdo, 2018.

Glaeser, Georg, et al. *The Evolution of Flight*. Springer International, 2017.

ONLINE RESOURCES

To learn more about the evolution of insects, visit **abdobooklinks.com**. These links are routinely monitored and updated to provide the most current information available.

MORE INFORMATION

For more information on this subject, contact or visit the following organizations:

CALIFORNIA ACADEMY OF SCIENCES

55 Music Concourse Dr.
San Francisco, CA 94118
415-379-8000
calacademy.org

Scientists at the California Academy of Sciences conduct research about evolution and insects.

SMITHSONIAN NATIONAL MUSEUM OF NATURAL HISTORY

Tenth St. and Constitution Ave. NW
Washington, DC 20560
202-633-1000
naturalhistory.si.edu

The National Museum of Natural History includes an insect zoo.

SOURCE NOTES

CHAPTER 1. INCREDIBLE INSECTS

1. "Entomology: Classification of Insects." *Royal Entomological*, 2016, royensoc.co.uk. Accessed 14 Sept. 2018.

2. "BugInfo: Numbers of Insects (Species and Individuals)." *Smithsonian*, n.d., si.edu. Accessed 14 Sept. 2018.

3. "Eurypterida: 'Sea Scorpions.'" *University of California Museum of Paleontology*, n.d., ucmp.berkeley.edu. Accessed 14 Sept. 2018.

4. "Geological Background." *The Burgess Shale*, 2011, burgess-shale.rom.on.ca. Accessed 14 Sept. 2018.

5. Kate Yandell. "Genetic Data Clarify Insect Evolution." *The Scientist*, 6 Nov. 2014, the-scientist.com. Accessed 14 Sept. 2018.

6. "BugInfo: Numbers of Insects."

CHAPTER 2. DRAGONFLIES AND DAMSELFLIES

1. "Dragonfly." *Encyclopædia Britannica*, 2 Aug. 2018, britannica.com. Accessed 14 Sept. 2018.

2. David Grimaldi and Michael S. Engel. *Evolution of the Insects*. Cambridge UP, 2006. 169-170.

3. Robert L. Carlton. *A Concise Dictionary of Paleontology*. Springer, 2018. 207. *Google Books*. Accessed 14 Sept. 2018.

4. Grimaldi and Engel, *Evolution of the Insects*, 169–170.

5. Asher Elbein. "Insects Flew Before Anything Else Did. So How Did They Get Their Wings?" *New York Times*, 26 Mar. 2018, nytimes.com. Accessed 14 Sept. 2018.

6. Vasika Udurawane. "The Biggest Insect Ever Was a Huge 'Dragonfly.'" *Earth Archives*, 2016, eartharchives.org. Accessed 14 Sept. 2018.

7. Ker Than. "Giant Bugs Eaten out of Existence by First Birds?" *National Geographic*, 18 June 2012, nationalgeographic.com. Accessed 14 Sept. 2018.

8. Brad Plumer. "There Have Been Five Mass Extinctions in Earth's History. Now We're Facing a Sixth." *Washington Post*, 11 Feb. 2014, washingtonpost.com. Accessed 14 Sept. 2018.

9. Christoph Benisch. "Phylogeny of the Beetles." *Beetle Fauna of Germany*, 2010, kerbtier.de. Accessed 14 Sept. 2018.

CHAPTER 3. COCKROACHES, TERMITES, AND MANTISES

1. "Cockroach." *Encyclopædia Britannica*, 23 Aug. 2018, britannica.com. Accessed 14 Sept. 2018.

2. Niki Wilson. "Why Termites Build Such Enormous Skyscrapers." *BBC*, 10 Dec. 2015, bbc.com. Accessed 14 Sept. 2018.

3. "Praying Mantis." *National Geographic*, 2018, nationalgeographic.com. Accessed 14 Sept. 2018.

4. University of Sydney. "How Cathedral Termites Got to Australia to Build Their 'Sky-Scrapers.'" *ScienceDaily*, 21 Feb. 2017, sciencedaily.com. Accessed 14 Sept. 2018.

5. "Facts & Figures." *Burj Khalifa*, n.d., burjkhalifa.ae. Accessed 14 Sept. 2018.

6. Charles Q. Choi. "Termites Are Actually Social Cockroaches." *LiveScience*, 11 Jan. 2008. Accessed 14 Sept. 2018.

7. Jes Rust and Torsten Wappler. "Palaeontology: The Point of No Return in the Fossil Record of Eusociality." *Current Biology*, vol. 26, no. 4, 2016, sciencedirect.com. Accessed 14 Sept. 2018.

CHAPTER 4. BEETLES

1. "Beetle Gallery." *National Insect Week*, 2018, nationalinsectweek.co.uk. Accessed 14 Sept. 2018.

2. Judson Linsley Gressitt. "Coleopteran." *Encyclopædia Britannica*, 23 Feb. 2018, britannica.com/animal/beetle. Accessed 14 Sept. 2018.

3. "Featured Creatures: Common Name: Featherwing Beetles." *University of Florida and the Florida Department of Agriculture and Consumer Services*, n.d., entnemdept.ufl.edu. Accessed 14 Sept. 2018.

4. "Largest Species of Beetle." *Guinness World Records*, 2018, guinnessworldrecords.com. Accessed 14 Sept. 2018.

5. Ferris Jabr. "How Did Insect Metamorphosis Evolve?" *Scientific American*, 10 Aug. 2012. Accessed 14 Sept. 2018.

6. Jana Goyens et al. "Cost of Flight and the Evolution of Stag Beetle Weaponry." *Journal of The Royal Society Interface*, vol. 12, no. 106, 15 Apr. 2015, rsif.royalsocietypublishing.org. Accessed 14 Sept. 2018.

CHAPTER 5. BUTTERFLIES AND MOTHS

1. Katie Pavid. "Butterfly Wings: The Science behind the Colour." *Natural History Museum*, 16 Jan. 2016, nhm.ac.uk. Accessed 14 Sept. 2018.

2. Jason Bittel. "Monarch Butterflies Migrate 3,000 Miles—Here's How." *National Geographic*, 17 Oct. 2017, news.nationalgeographic.com. Accessed 14 Sept. 2018.

3. Sana Suri. "Despite Metamorphosis, Moths Hold On to Memories from Their Days as a Caterpillar." *The Conversation*, 29 Mar. 2018, theconversation.com. Accessed 14 Sept. 2018.

4. Carl Zimmer. "Ten Great Advances in Evolution." *PBS*, 26 Oct. 2009, pbs.org. Accessed 14 Sept. 2018.

CHAPTER 6. FLIES AND FLEAS

1. Harold Oldroyd. "Dipteran." *Encyclopædia Britannica*, 13 Oct. 2017, britannica.com. Accessed 14 Sept. 2018.

2. North Carolina State University. "'Fly Tree of Life' Mapped, Adds Big Branch of Evolutionary Knowledge." *ScienceDaily*, 14 Mar. 2011, sciencedaily.com. Accessed 14 Sept. 2018.

3. "Flea: Learn More About Flea." *ScienceDirect*, 2018, sciencedirect.com. Accessed 14 Sept. 2018.

4. Robert Traub and Miriam Louisa Rothschild. "Flea." *Encyclopædia Britannica*, 11 Jan. 2018, britannica.com. Accessed 14 Sept. 2018.

5. "Fruit Fly Gene Success." *BBC News*, 18 Feb. 2000, bbc.co.uk. Accessed 14 Sept. 2018.

6. Markham Heid. "You Asked: Do Fruit Flies Come from Inside Fruit?" *Time*, 15 Oct. 2018, time.com. Accessed 14 Sept. 2018.

7. Robin McKie. "Six Nobel Prizes–What's the Fascination with the Fruit Fly?" *Guardian*, 7 Oct. 2017, theguardian.com. Accessed 14 Sept. 2018.

8. Claire Bates. "Would It Be Wrong to Eradicate Mosquitoes?" *BBC News*, 28 Jan. 2016, bbc.com. Accessed 14 Sept. 2018.

9. Erin Blakemore. "The London Underground Has Its Own Mosquito Subspecies." *Smithsonian.com*, 25 Mar. 2016, smithsonianmag.com. Accessed Sept. 2018.

10. Stephanie Pappas. "Giant Bloodsuckers! Oldest Fleas Discovered." *LiveScience*, 29 Feb. 2012, livescience.com. Accessed 14 Sept. 2018.

11. Tia Ghose. "Sneaky Ancient Flea Dined on Flying Reptiles." *LiveScience*, 27 June 2013, livescience.com. Accessed 14 Sept. 2018.

CHAPTER 7. BEES, WASPS, AND ANTS

1. Seraina Klopfstein et al. "The Hymenopteran Tree of Life: Evidence from Protein-Coding Genes and Objectively Aligned Ribosomal Data." *PLoS ONE*, vol. 8, no. 8, 2 Aug. 2013, journals.plos.org. Accessed 14 Sept. 2018.

2. Michael G. Brandstetter et al. "Phylogenomic Insights into the Evolution of Stinging Wasps and the Origins of Ants and Bees." *Current Biology*, vol. 27, no. 7, 3 Apr. 2017, cell.com. Accessed 14 Sept. 2018.

3. Krishna Ramanujan. "Study Settles Debate over Origins of Ants and Bees." *Phys.org*, 26 Aug. 2017, phys.org. Accessed 14 Sept. 2018.

4. Carl Zimmer. "Key to Ants' Evolution May Have Started With a Wasp." *New York Times*, 17 Oct. 2013, nytimes.com. Accessed 14 Sept. 2018.

5. Joanna Klein. "How Ants Figured Out Farming Millions of Years Before Humans." *New York Times*, 11 Apr. 2017, nytimes.com. Accessed 14 Sept. 2018.

CHAPTER 8. GRASSHOPPERS, CRICKETS, AND KATYDIDS

1. John P. Roche. "The Origin of Grasshoppers, Katydids, and Crickets: A New Study Resolves the Evolutionary Tree of the Orthoptera." *Entomology Today*, 8 Apr. 2015, entomologytoday.org. Accessed 14 Sept. 2018.

2. "Cricket." *Encyclopædia Britannica*, 19 Sept. 2017, britannica.com. Accessed 14 Sept. 2018.

3. Kara Rogers. "Katydid." *Encyclopædia Britannica*, 11 Feb. 2015, britannica.com. Accessed 14 Sept. 2018.

4. "Grasshopper." *Encyclopædia Britannica*, 22 Sept. 2017, britannica.com. Accessed 14 Sept. 2018.

5. Goggy Davidowitz. "Grasshoppers." *Arizona-Sonora Desert Museum*, 2018, desertmuseum.org. Accessed 14 Sept. 2018.

6. David Attenborough. *Life in the Undergrowth*. Princeton UP, 2005. 84–85.

7. "Quick Evolution Leads to Quiet Crickets." *University of California, Berkeley: Understanding Evolution*, May 2016, evolution.berkeley.edu. Accessed 14 Sept. 2018.

8. Mindy Weisberger. "Cicadas Are Coming! Brood VI Returns After 17 Years." *LiveScience*, 12 June 2017, livescience.com. Accessed 14 Sept. 2018.

9. Cayte Bosler. "To Save the World, Eat Bugs." *Atlantic*, 25 Feb. 2014, theatlantic.com. Accessed 14 Sept. 2018.

CHAPTER 9. RESEARCH TODAY

1. "Images of 300 Million-Year-Old Insects Revealed." *University of Manchester*, 26 Mar. 2012, manchester.ac.uk. Accessed 14 Sept. 2018.

2. "Scientists Resolve the Evolution of Insects." *Natural History Museum*, 11 Mar. 2015, nhm.ac.uk. Accessed 14 Sept. 2018.

3. Nicholas St. Fleur. "After Dinosaur Extinction, Some Insects Recovered More Quickly." *New York Times*, 17 Nov. 2016, nytimes.com. Accessed 14 Sept. 2018.

INDEX

ABOUT THE AUTHOR

Christine Evans is a children's author living in Northern California with her husband and daughters. When she's not writing, she's enjoying the great outdoors, exploring nature with her kids, hugging redwood trees, and running local trails. Ever since an elementary school project on the life cycle of butterflies, she has adored them—her favorite is the peacock butterfly. Christine is originally from the United Kingdom, where they call ladybugs ladybirds.